P9-CBF-523

DISCARD

WEST GEORGIA REGIONAL LIBRARY SYSTEM
Neva Lomason Memorial Library

GREAT MYSTERIES

The Lost Colony of Roanoke

OPPOSING VIEWPOINTS

Look for these and other exciting *Great Mysteries: Opposing Viewpoints* books:

GREAT MYSTERIES
The Lost Colony of Roanoke

OPPOSING VIEWPOINTS

by Tom Schouweiler

Greenhaven Press, Inc.   P.O. Box 289009, San Diego, California 92198-0009

No part of this book may be reproduced or used in any form or by any means, electrical, mechanical, or otherwise, including, but not limited to, photocopy, recording, or any information storage and retrieval system, without prior written permission from the publisher.

Library of Congress Cataloging-in-Publication Data

Schouweiler, Tom, 1965-
    The lost colony of Roanoke : opposing viewpoints / by Thomas Schouweiler.
       p.   cm.—(Great mysteries)
    Includes bibliographical references and index.
    Summary: Presents opposing viewpoints about the mysterious disappearance of the English colony on Roanoke Island.
    ISBN 0-89908-093-6 (lib. bdg.)
    1. Roanoke Colony (N.C.)—Juvenile literature.   [1. Roanoke Colony (N.C.)]
I. Title. II. Series: Great mysteries
F229.S246   1991
975.6'175—dc20   91-15188

© Copyright 1991 by Greenhaven Press, Inc.

for
Grace Mary Grady
my favorite librarian

Contents

Introduction

This book is written for the curious—those who want to explore the mysteries that are everywhere. To be human is to be constantly surrounded by wonderment. How do birds fly? Are ghosts real? Can animals and people communicate? Was King Arthur a real person or a myth? Why did Amelia Earhart disappear? Did history really happen the way we think it did? Where did the world come from? Where is it going?

Great Mysteries: Opposing Viewpoints books are intended to offer the reader an opportunity to explore some of the many mysteries that both trouble and intrigue us. For the span of each book, we want the reader to feel that he or she is a scientist investigating the extinction of the dinosaurs, an archaeologist searching for clues to the origin of the great Egyptian pyramids, a psychic detective testing the existence of ESP.

One thing all mysteries have in common is that there is no ready answer. Often there are *many* answers but none on which even the majority of authorities agrees. *Great Mysteries: Opposing Viewpoints* books introduce the intriguing views of the experts, allowing the reader to participate in their explorations, their theories, and their disagreements as they try to explain the mysteries of our world.

But most readers won't want to stop here. These *Great Mysteries: Opposing Viewpoints* aim to stimulate the reader's curiosity. Although truth is often impossible to discover, the search is fascinating. It is up to the reader to examine the evidence, to decide whether the answer is there—or to explore further.

"Penetrating so many secrets, we cease to believe in the unknowable. But there it sits nevertheless, calmly licking its chops."

H.L. Mencken, American essayist

Prologue

Distant Smoke

On the fifteenth of August, 1590, John White recorded in his journal that the crews of his fleet of three ships "saw a great smoke rise in the Isle Roanoke near the place where I left our colony in the year 1587."

White, governor of the colony, was returning with supplies and reinforcements after a three-year absence. When he left, he promised he would be back the following spring. But history intervened and war with Spain delayed his return to Roanoke Island. The remainder of the journal entry expressed his anticipation at the prospect of being reunited with his colony and his relief that its people appeared to be all right, as indicated by the smoke from what he thought were their fires. For White knew many dangers faced the colony in this new land, called Virginia by the English.

Announcing Their Arrival

It was late in the day when White and his company sighted the smoke, so they waited until the next day to announce their arrival. On the morning of the sixteenth, the ship fired off three cannons for the colonists to hear. A member of White's company sighted smoke again, this time on the mainland, farther down the sandy coast from the place

(opposite page) In this nineteenth-century lithograph, Sir Walter Raleigh and his men meet with natives on the shore of Roanoke Island.

the colony should have been. White decided to investigate that site first. His crew misjudged how far away the smoke was. They marched a long time, until they "were very sore tired," before reaching their destination. White wrote, "When we came to the smoke we found no man nor sign that any had been there lately." They had marched all day without any drinking water only to discover no more than the remnants of a small brush fire, common to the area.

The Site of the Colony

They located fresh water and returned to their ship, determined to go to the site of the colony on Roanoke Island the next morning.

At ten A.M., White and his crew took the smaller boats into the shallow harbor. Unluckily, a storm suddenly blew up, nearly capsizing the boats and ruining the supplies they had brought. Nonetheless,

Gov. John White and crew ferry supplies ashore to Roanoke Island. A sudden storm nearly capsized their boat.

they managed to land on the island. They stood on the beach and played a trumpet and sang familiar English folk songs to reassure the colony they were a friendly party. But no response came from inside the dark forest of cedar trees.

No English Footprints

Governor White wrote: "We returned by the waterside round about the north point of the island, until we came to the place where I left our colony in the year 1587. In all this way we saw in the sand the print of the savages' [natives'] feet." They found no footprints made by English shoes.

White expected to see the 113 people, including his daughter and granddaughter, he had left behind. What he found instead was a lone cryptic clue. On a tree, wrote White, "were curiously carved these fair Roman letters C R O."

Later, on another part of the island, he found a tree with the whole word CROATOAN carved in it.

White and the colonists had agreed, before he left in 1587, that if they should relocate they would carve the name of their destination into a tree. They had also agreed that if they should leave in haste or distress they would carve a Maltese cross next to the destination. Since no cross was carved, White assumed that the colonists had not left in distress.

Thus he was reassured that they were at Croatoan, "the place where Manteo was born and the savages . . . our friends." Manteo was a native of the Croatoan area who had spent time in England and acted as a link between the two cultures.

A Sudden Gale

Although White thought it strange for the colonists to move south of the original site, he assumed they had good reason to do as they did. He prepared to set sail for Croatoan, anticipating the reunion that had been delayed for three years.

Nature again worked against the governor. A

"The City of Raleigh was to become another Bristol, Southampton, or Plymouth; a solid and prosperous trading port."

Raleigh biographer Robert Lacey

"We found no man nor sign that any had been there lately."

John White, from his journal of 1590

Gov. John White and others find "CROATOAN" carved into the bark of a tree. White assumed the message meant the colonists were with friendly natives at Croatoan.

sudden gale blew up and dangerously battered the ships. The chain of an anchor being raised on White's vessel broke, injuring several sailors. A second anchor was lost in an attempt to prevent the ship from going aground and sinking. One anchor remained. Mooring off the Virginia coast with its shallow shoreline and unpredictable storms would now be too dangerous. As the gale blew the ships east, White decided to head back to England.

The Colonists Disappear

It was to be John White's last attempt to contact the colonists he left on Roanoke Island in 1587. The founder of the expedition, Sir Walter Raleigh, was having trouble back in England and no longer had the time or money to dedicate to the effort.

The colonists—men, women, and children who had left England in hope of a better life in the strange new land—were never heard from again. They had disappeared. Their fates and that of their lost colony remains a mystery.

One

Bitter Rivalry

(opposite page) Natives were living in well-structured, organized villages when the English colonists arrived in the New World.

Since the beginning of the sixteenth century, tensions between Spain and England had been increasing at a steady rate. One cause was Spain's successful exploration of the New World. In fact, by the time the English made their attempt to colonize Roanoke Island off the coast of present-day North Carolina, the Spanish had already explored, settled, and claimed as their own much of South, Central, and North America.

In 1521, a Spanish explorer named Francisco de Gordillo landed off the coast of what is now South Carolina. Five years later, a justice of the Spanish supreme court named Allyon conducted an expedition from Florida up the eastern seaboard of the United States. Allyon traveled as far as the area that some eighty years later would become the English colony of Jamestown, Virginia. There Allyon's group tried to establish a colony, but fever and attacks by natives weakened them and they abandoned the settlement. In 1525, a Portuguese ship pilot named Estevan Gomez landed on the east coast of Canada north of Maine. The exploits of these three early explorers enabled Spain by 1526 to claim the entire eastern seaboard of what is now the United States.

"For the people [of England, conflict with Spain] was a struggle of the Reformation [the Protestant church] against the Papacy [the Catholic Church]."

Sir Julian S. Corbett, British historian

"English seamen like Raleigh would . . . make themselves rich men in the process [of fighting Spain]."

Raleigh biographer Robert Lacey

The Spanish also discovered, explored, and claimed large parts of the interior of the United States and Mexico. In 1528, Panfilo de Navarez and a company of eighty reached present-day Texas. Ten years later, the Spanish had reached the Pacific Ocean in California. Around that same time, Hernando de Soto discovered, explored, and made many expeditions up the Mississippi River until finally, in 1542, it became his grave.

Wild rumors of cities built of gold in the southern region of this new continent inspired Francisco de Coronado and his party of three hundred to seek those cities. What they found instead were the pueblo villages of the American Southwest. They also discovered the Grand Canyon. On this extensive 1540 expedition, they covered territory that is now Mexico, Texas, Oklahoma, New Mexico, and Kansas.

By 1556, Spain had claimed the land all the way from the Strait of Magellan at the tip of South America north to central Mexico, and all the mainland of the present-day U.S. from the Atlantic to the Pacific Ocean. The English found Spain's claims in the New World distressing because Spain and England were old enemies. England wanted some of the New World, too.

Tensions grew with each passing year. During the period the colony at Roanoke was established, this tension broke out into war between the two countries.

Outbreak of War

War between England and the more powerful Spanish nation came as no surprise. The two powers had long harbored hostilities in three major areas: religious, political, and economic.

For most of the people of England, the conflict was a religious one, according to Sir Julian S. Corbett, a turn-of-the-century British history scholar. In the 1580s, Spain was under the rule of the Catholic

King Philip, while the queen of England, Elizabeth, was a Protestant. This was a time of terrible conflict between these two Christian sects. Members of the Protestant religion were often persecuted and tortured in Catholic Spain, and Catholics were treated the same way in England. Both countries believed that the religion of their ruler was the one true religion. Both saw the other religion as an affront to God that must be abolished.

Spain Versus England

For English politicians, the conflict with Spain arose out of England's wish to assert influence on an international scene dominated by Spain. Spain's navy was the strongest in the world, and it was obvious that King Philip intended someday to conquer England with it. The politicians of England wished to put a stop to what they saw as Spanish military aggression. They also wanted to make England the dominant military and naval force in the world. Not only would such a move make England stronger, it would increase England's wealth through greater trade opportunities.

Economically, the merchants of England hated Spain because Spain's military might reduced English trade opportunities. Spain had such a strong hold on the seas that they controlled sea trade. This prevented English merchants from operating in some places. If England dominated the sea, then English merchants would be able to trade with more people and make much more money.

The political and economic motives went together. It took money to build ships, and it took ships to establish a strong navy to dominate the seas and make increased trade possible.

In his book *Imperial Spain*, assistant professor Edward D. Salmon of Amherst College states that England had earnestly begun building its naval fleet since the first half of the sixteenth century, the reign of King Henry VIII, in order to take dominance of

King Philip (above) ruled Spain in the 1580s. His rivalry with and distrust of the English monarchy eventually led to war between the nations.

King Henry VIII of England wanted total naval superiority over Spain.

the sea away from the Spanish. The way the English paid for this increase in shipbuilding was called privateering.

Pirate Profits

Rich merchants or politicians, sometimes even the queen, would invest money to buy ships and hire crews to sail out into the Atlantic Ocean. These privateers would sail south between Spain and its colonies in the Caribbean looking for ships filled with valuable supplies and resources from the New World. The English ships were small and fast and had large guns. The Spanish supply ships were old, larger, and much heavier because they were fully laden with goods, and they did not have large guns. Usually it was easy for the English to take a Spanish ship by force and return to England with it. The ships were generally filled with spices or valuable furs and skins from the New World. In England, the contents of the Spanish ship would be sold, and each investor in the expedition would receive a share of the profits. Usually the profit was many times what he or she had invested. The man who

This and other Spanish ships carried spices, furs, precious metals, and other goods from the New World to Spain.

would found the first English colonies at Roanoke, Sir Walter Raleigh, obtained most of his great wealth through privateering expeditions.

The Importance of a Colony

Raleigh believed it important for the English to establish a colony in the New World. He argued to Queen Elizabeth that a colony halfway up the east coast of America would be an ideal spot for the English to conduct military privateering expeditions against Spanish ships. The English ships could leave the colony and sail the relatively short distance down to the Caribbean. There they could commandeer Spanish ships filled with valuable commodities as they left their colonies. The English could then make the easy voyage back up the coast rather than risk a dangerous trip across the Atlantic Ocean where they might be destroyed by storms or Spanish warships. Raleigh thought that in addition to being profitable, these activities could be advantageous politically. He once wrote about the king of Spain, "If you touch Philip [in the Caribbean], you touch the apple of his eye, for you take away his treasure."

Another reason to establish a colony was that both the English and the Spanish were looking for the Northwest Passage. It was widely believed at the time that there must be a water route through the mainland of America to the Pacific Ocean and Japan, China, and India. We know today that there is no such thing. That is why the Panama Canal was built in the early twentieth century. But these sixteenth-century Europeans had very little idea of how vast North and South America were. Sir Walter Raleigh argued that a colony would enable the English to search for and hopefully discover the passage and claim it for England. Such a claim would give England great wealth by providing easy access to a large market for trade in the Orient. Oriental and Indian spices and clothes were highly valued in Eu-

Sir Walter Raleigh explored and claimed the New World on behalf of Queen Elizabeth of England (below).

rope at that time.

Raleigh also told the queen that the colonists could spread the Protestant religion among the natives of the New World and that unemployed English people could be sent to work in this new land to create wealth for England.

Because he was so persuasive and also because the queen liked Raleigh especially well, Elizabeth gave him the right to explore and claim the New World on her behalf. In the spring of 1584, she asked him to:

> discover, search, find out, and view such remote, heathen, and barbarous lands, countries, and territories, not actually possessed of any Christian prince, nor inhabited by Christian people.

And so Raleigh began organizing an expedition to colonize the New World in order to stop Spanish aggression against England, spread the Protestant religion, and make himself a wealthy man.

Raleigh was an amazing man of many talents and interests. He was a poet, politician, writer, and privateer, and in 1584 he became a colonizer of North America, though he never journeyed there himself.

Sir Walter Raleigh

Walter Raleigh was born in the English county of Devon around the year 1552. His family was not wealthy, but they had enough money to send him to Oriel College in Oxford.

At seventeen, he fought in France for the cause of Protestantism. In 1577, he fought against the Spanish in the Netherlands. Because of his outstanding record on the battlefield and his considerable personal charm, he became a favorite of Queen Elizabeth in the 1580s.

He supported the queen's domestic and foreign policies. In return, she granted him rights to trade both inside and outside of England. This enabled him to become wealthy.

Sir Walter Raleigh was a fierce and loyal fighter. His support of Queen Elizabeth allowed him free reign in trade. As a result, he became a wealthy man.

The queen knighted him in 1584, making him *Sir* Walter Raleigh. Shortly after that, the queen granted him the right to explore, claim, and exploit the natural resources of the New World.

Stripped of His Wealth

Raleigh's many conflicts with the Spanish navy began with his privateering activities upon their merchant ships. He also fought the Spanish navy in military battles, the most notable of which was when he sailed against the Spanish Armada in the summer of 1588. This was the same time period that he was most heavily involved in the colonizing efforts at Roanoke. It was also a high point in royal favor toward Raleigh.

Although Raleigh lost the queen's favor briefly when he married one of her assistants, he retained a close friendship with the monarch until she died in 1603. Unfortunately for Raleigh, her successor, King James, disliked him so much that he was stripped of all his wealth and jailed in the Tower of London. Raleigh was freed in March of 1616 to search for gold in South America. When he came back empty handed he was executed.

Raleigh was a controversial figure during his lifetime. He was strongly loved and strongly hated. Perhaps his greatest achievement was his efforts that led the English to try to colonize the New World. His personal efforts created a widespread interest in the new lands across the Atlantic. For instance, when the first colonists brought back tobacco, never before seen in Europe, Raleigh adopted the habit of smoking. Due to his colorful and popular personality, smoking became a popular pastime among English nobility.

Through his efforts to plant settlements in North America in the 1580s, Raleigh paved the way for later successful colonies. One of his first efforts was to arrange an exploratory expedition in the spring of 1584. Although the company did not establish a

Raleigh's wife visits her husband after he is jailed in the Tower of London by King James.

Many Native Americans decorated themselves with feathers and other ornaments. They wore their hair long, tying it in a knot close to their ears.

colony, some historians believe the actions of this expedition influenced the fate of the lost colonists.

The expedition consisted of a fleet of two ships under the guidance of captains Arthur Barlowe and Philip Amadas. A Portuguese sailor named Simao Fernandes steered the ships. Fernandes had made many previous voyages to North America and would later deliver the lost colonists there.

After three months at sea the 1584 expedition landed off the coast of present-day North Carolina. Impressed by the abundance of the land and the friendliness of its natives, Barlowe named the land Virginia after Queen Elizabeth, who was called the Virgin Queen. At that time, Virginia extended from what is now South Carolina to Massachusetts and Maine. The present state of Virginia is only a small portion of this area.

The English enjoyed good relations with the natives and traded goods for food and animal pelts. In the autumn when the English needed to return to England, they persuaded two natives, Manteo and Wanchese, to make the voyage with them.

The First Colony at Roanoke

With the knowledge gained from one voyage, Raleigh felt ready to establish a permanent settlement in the New World. He originally envisioned fifteen ships laden with ample supplies and around

The colonists and natives met in villages like this, trading European goods for animal pelts and food.

three hundred soldier-colonists. He would include specialists in every field to deal with any circumstance—mineral experts, a blacksmith, bakers, tile makers, barbers, weavers, and even a man who was especially adept at making eyelet holes in canvas. No women would be among the group as the untamed wilderness of the New World was considered too dangerous.

Unfortunately, these ambitious plans exceeded the amount of money Raleigh was able to raise. The queen's loss of interest in the venture was particularly harmful to his plans. Thus, in April 1585, only seven ships left England bound for Virginia's Outer Banks, the chain of long, narrow, sandy islands that runs along the coast. The expedition was headed by Sir Richard Grenville, a career navy man and cousin of Raleigh. Ralph Lane, a twenty-five-year-old favorite of the queen adept at fort making, was to be the governor of the colonists once they arrived in

In April 1585, the New World's first permanent English settlers left England on board seven ships. They sailed for the islands off the coast of Virginia.

Virginia. Simao Fernandes was again in charge of piloting the principal ship of the expedition. Also along were John White, an artist and mapmaker, Manteo, and Wanchese.

Off the coast of Portugal, the fleet encountered a storm that sank one of the smaller ships and scattered the fleet. Because the ships had no way of communicating with each other except visual signals, Fernandes, Grenville, and Lane did not know whether the other ships had sunk or not. They had no choice but to hope for the best and continue sailing. They took the usual route: south to the Canary Islands off Africa and then straight west to the Caribbean Islands and finally northward to Virginia.

Fernandes steered the main ship to Puerto Rico, where the captains had agreed to meet if the ships became separated. Since their stay in that place deep in the heart of Spanish territory would be of unknown length, Grenville decided to use Lane's expertise to build a fort. Inside the fort the men built another ship to replace one that had been lost in the storm.

Grenville's company encountered a small Spanish force but outnumbered it. The Spanish would not be a threat as long as the English left before reinforcements arrived. After about three weeks, all but one of the missing ships were reunited with the fleet, and on May 19, 1585, the adventurers burned their fort down and left the island.

One reason English ships sailed through Spanish territory rather than straight across the Atlantic was the chance for privateering opportunities. Privateering was the easiest way to pay for the expensive new colony. Grenville was quite lucky in this respect, capturing four richly laden Spanish vessels.

The fleet continued to the island of Hispaniola, another Spanish possession. Because the English fleet was so large, it was in no danger from the Spanish there. Grenville arranged for the colonists

"We returned . . . to Aquascogoc to demand a silver cup which one of the savages had stolen from us. Not receiving it according to . . . promise, we burnt and spoiled their corn and town, all the people being fled."

Sir Richard Grenville

"[By destroying Aquascogoc,] the scouts had stored up trouble for the future."

Raleigh biographer Robert Lacey

to obtain some needed supplies to replace those lost on the ship that sank off Portugal. To get these supplies he traded goods to the Spanish that he had pirated from them only days earlier!

At the end of June the fleet arrived off the coast of Virginia. These waters are very difficult to navigate even today, and Fernandes ran one of the ships aground and all its supplies were ruined.

Finding a Site

A search party including Grenville and Lane took a small ship called a pinnace to look for a suitable place to establish the colony. They passed through many native villages where they were welcomed. All of these villages were in the domain of Chief Wingina, the brother of Granganimeo whom Amadas and Barlowe had met the previous year.

One such village was called Aquascogoc. At this place, while the English were being entertained, a silver cup belonging to one of the search party disappeared. Grenville assumed the worst. He demanded that the natives return the cup by the time he and his party got back from exploring the area. When the English returned a few days later the cup had not been found. Grenville ordered that the town and all the crops be burned down. No doubt Grenville's intention was to teach the "savage heathens" (his words) a lesson about the importance of native obedience to the conquering English. But the colonists would later find that the natives had learned two lessons. First, the English intended to dominate the area. Second, the English were not necessarily their friends.

After the encounter at Aquascogoc, the whole fleet moved up the coast to the place where Amadas and Barlowe had landed the previous year. There they were happily met by Granganimeo, who had not yet heard about the destruction of Aquascogoc. He offered part of the island Roanoke, where he sometimes lived, to the English as the site for their colony. After a brief inspection of the island, Grenville and Lane decided it was a suitable spot and began unloading food, cattle, and other supplies from the ships. One ship was sent back to England immediately to replace those supplies lost when Fernandes ran it aground.

Grenville decided that 108 men would be left at the colony. This was far short of the 800 men originally recommended for the venture and less than half of the 300 men Grenville had at his disposal. Historians do not know why he decided on this number, but they generally agree it was insufficient to begin a colony.

Preparing for Winter

In August 1585, Grenville left with the remainder of the fleet except for a pinnace to be used in exploration. He promised to return with reinforcements and supplies by the following Easter.

Under the guidance of Lane, the colonists began building a fort in preparation for the winter to come. This was easy to do on the heavily wooded island. The fort was small, about seventy feet square. The men built dormitory-style huts in the area between the fort and the native village. The fort sat on the northeast end of the island so it would be hidden from Spanish patrol vessels.

Being soldiers, the colonists made no effort to plant crops or learn the natives' agricultural techniques. They did not even learn their simple fishing methods that brought such high yields. Instead they relied on the seemingly endless goodwill of the natives.

This became a source of tension between the two groups after the colony's food supply was quickly consumed. It was difficult for the natives to support the colonists because, unlike Europeans, they did not grow excess crops for storage. Instead, the tribe grew only what they could eat, and when the growing season was over they would live on

To eat, the colonists relied on the goodwill of the natives, who prepared food for the colonists and themselves.

shellfish and game until the crops were ready again.

Tensions were increased by the fact that the Englishmen introduced diseases into the native community to which the natives had no resistance. Often, after the English visited a community, people would begin to die mysteriously. The unexplained sicknesses, the white skin of the Englishmen, and the strange European customs and devices caused some of the natives to think the colonists were of divine origin. These natives feared and respected the newcomers, but the respect was increasingly mixed with hostility.

Other natives saw little evidence that the white people were divine. They needed food like any other people. Furthermore, they seemed incapable of mastering the simple techniques involved in getting it. Chief Wingina seemed to waver in his opinion of the colonists at first, but by April 1586, he had tired of the demands of these decidedly human newcomers.

Besides establishing the first colony in the New World, Lane and his colonists had been charged with exploring the surrounding area. They were to locate a more suitable place for a permanent settlement, a place with a deep-water harbor. So in April, after the coldest part of winter was over, an expedition started up the Roanoke River to look for gold and a site for the future City of Raleigh.

Secret Messengers

Wingina pretended to be as helpful as always. He provided guides for this trip, as he usually did. But after Lane's men set out, Wingina secretly sent messengers ahead to tell the native villages along the river that the white skinned visitors were not friendly and meant to take their food, which, at the end of the winter, was scarce. Indeed, Lane and his crew carried with them only enough food for two days, assuming the natives would supply them along the way.

Lane sailed up the river and neither met any natives, nor in Lane's own words, found a single "grain of corn in any of their towns." Not attributing this strange absence of people and supplies to any deception on Wingina's part, the party pressed on. Meanwhile, back on Roanoke Island, Wingina told the remaining colonists that Lane and the crew had died of starvation on the river, as he expected they had. He also tried to persuade his own tribe to stop giving food to the colonists on the island so that they, too, would starve.

One hundred fifty miles away from Roanoke, Lane and his men ran out of food. That night, natives in the surrounding woods shot hundreds of arrows at the colonists in their boats. Surprisingly, no one was injured by the arrows, and gunfire from the English scared away the natives. The exploration party quickly decided that they would begin the return trip to Roanoke in the morning. They put out guard dogs that night in case the natives returned.

The dogs served double duty the next morning

Natives met among themselves, discussing white people. They agreed there was little proof of whites' divinity.

"[Ensenore, a native friendly to the first colony,] had sowed a good quantity of ground. So much as had been sufficient to have fed our whole company for a year. Besides that he gave us a certain plot of ground for ourselves to sow."

Ralph Lane, a member of Grenville's crew

"The local population [natives] did not farm on a European basis, producing a surplus with which they could trade and on which they could survive until the next harvest came along. . . . So it was difficult for them to support over a hundred hungry Europeans."

Raleigh biographer Robert Lacey

by becoming breakfast for the hungry crew. They figured that the dog stew would be enough to keep them alive for the journey back to Roanoke. They arrived three days later. It was the day after Easter, the day Grenville had promised to return with supplies and reinforcements. There were no ships to be seen on the horizon.

By this time, Lane had deduced that Wingina had tricked him. Wingina now moved his tribe inland and stopped all supplies to the colonists. Information obtained from a captured native led Lane to believe that Wingina was plotting to kill him, John White, and the other leaders of the colony by setting their huts afire. The natives would then beat them to death as they emerged from the conflagration, sleepy and confused.

Firing on the Natives

Lane decided the English should attack first, and on June 1, 1585, that is what they did. They went to Wingina's inland camp on the dubious pretense of journeying to meet the fleet from England. When they arrived, they fired on the natives, killing many. Wingina pretended to be shot, then jumped up and ran into the woods. Lane's personal servant, a man named Edward Nugent, shot Wingina in the left buttock and chased him. Nugent later emerged from the woods with the chief's head in his hands.

Lane and his men won the battle, but did they lose the war? At the very least, relations could never return to the mutual trust and friendship of earlier times. Today some historians believe that the brutal treatment of Wingina and his people may have contributed to the later disappearance of the lost colonists of Roanoke.

Sir Francis Drake, like Sir Walter Raleigh, was a successful privateer. In the spring of 1585 he was in Spanish territory in the Caribbean enjoying great success. As a privateer, he also realized the benefits of having an English colony on the east coast of

North America. Having heard of the colonists on Roanoke Island, he determined to visit them and offer his help if it was needed.

English or Spanish?

On June 8, 1585, the colonists spotted Drake's fleet. Desperate and starving after their troubles with the natives, they lit signal fires even though they were not sure if the ships were English or Spanish. They must have reasoned that capture by the Spanish would be preferable to death by starvation.

The ships were Drake's, however, and he was generous to the colonists. After hearing their tale of bad luck, he offered them a choice of passage back to England or ships and supplies. Though the future of the colony must have looked bleak, the colonists

Sir Francis Drake was generous to the starving, desperate colonists. He offered them passage back to England or, if they chose to stay, ships and supplies.

Leading the 1585 expedition to the New World was Sir Richard Grenville, a career navy man and a cousin to Sir Walter Raleigh.

decided to stay. Sick and unfit colonists were put on Drake's ships, and some of Drake's sailors decided to stay at the settlement. Two small ships that would remain with the colony were loaded with supplies.

Fierce storms arise quickly in that area. On June 13, "there arose a great storm," wrote Drake in his journal. It lasted three days, and the larger vessels were forced to put to sea or risk crashing on the rocks. Smaller vessels with the colony's supplies were wrecked. The sailors with Drake's fleet reconsidered and no longer wished to stay at the colony.

Drake again offered Lane and his people a choice: one ship filled with supplies or passage to England.

Demoralized by starvation, war with the natives, and lack of communication or support from Raleigh and Grenville, the colonists decided to abandon Roanoke Island and return to England.

A Ship Arrives

Only days after they left, a supply ship sent by Raleigh arrived. Finding the colony deserted, it returned to England. A larger fleet of thirty ships commanded by Grenville arrived about the middle of July. Grenville searched the area and questioned some natives until he got a general idea of what had happened and where the colonists had gone. Unwilling to give up English claim to the territory, he left fifteen men and supplies on the island until another colony could be established. Why he thought fifteen men could accomplish what more than one hundred could not is another of the mysteries surrounding the colonization efforts on Roanoke Island. Perhaps Grenville's desire to have an English colony in North America clouded his judgment.

Grenville returned to England to organize another attempt at colonization of the New World.

The next year, 1587, another group of English people set out for Roanoke Island. These colonists, under the governorship of John White, would suffer an even gloomier fate than that of Grenville's party. They were to become the lost colonists of Roanoke. —

Two

A City Is Founded

(opposite page) In this nineteenth-century engraving, Sir Walter Raleigh and his crew plant the flag of Queen Elizabeth on a Virginia beach, symbolizing England's colonization of the New World.

Despite the failures of the first colony, Sir Walter Raleigh was anxious to try again to settle the New World with English people. The largest problem with the first colony had been that Lane's men were soldiers, not settlers. They were paid the same whether the colony thrived or withered. Also, they were separated from their families and no doubt never felt truly at home in the New World.

This problem was solved by having whole families go on the next expedition. Brave householders sold everything they had in England to buy a share of Raleigh's holdings in the New World. They gambled all for a chance at a better life. Since they had nothing to return to, they would work hard to make the settlement succeed.

A second problem facing the would-be colonists was the unsuitability of Roanoke Island as a site. The treacherous seas had beached and sunk many ships there. If an English settlement in the New World was to be used as a base for privateering against the Spanish, huge ships had to be able to move in and out of a harbor with ease.

Fortunately, Lane had discovered and briefly explored a nearby deep-water bay called Chesepiock by the natives. Today it is known as Chesa-

peake Bay. It was well suited for the purposes of the English privateers.

A document signed on January 7, 1587, created a governing body called "the governor and assistants of the City of Raleigh in Virginia." John White, the illustrator and mapmaker from Grenville's voyage, was appointed as the governor.

Little is known about White's background except that he was trained as a surveyor. He had first visited the New World in 1577 on an expedition to Greenland and Baffin Island. There he drew informative sketches of the lands and natives the adventurers encountered.

Only one of the twelve assistants of the City of Raleigh had been across the Atlantic before. That was Simao Fernandes, the Portuguese pilot of Grenville's expedition. Another assistant was Ananias Dare, who was married to White's daughter.

Also along was the native Manteo, who had spent his second winter in England. He was still friendly with the English despite the slaughter at Aquascogoc. Manteo adopted many English ways

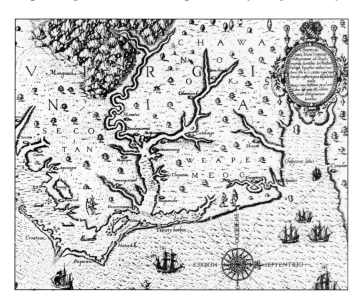

An early map of the Virginia colony and Chesapeake Bay.

while Wanchese had preferred to rejoin his people.

On May 5, 1587, eighty-five men, seventeen women, and eleven children boarded the ships heading for the New World. They were fourteen families, and two of the women, including Governor White's daughter, were pregnant. This shows that these people very much intended to settle in the new colony.

By the time the three ships left Plymouth, England, it was later than usual to begin such a journey. But White reckoned that the group had time enough because they would do no privateering until the colony was set up on Chesapeake Bay. Valuable time would not be lost waiting for Spanish prey to come along.

About a week after their embarkation, the two main ships were separated from the smaller ship during bad weather off the coast of Portugal. White feared the worst. The pilot of that ship had never been to the New World, so his chances of finding the way to the colony by himself were slim. This incident was the first to cause friction between the governor of the colony, White, and Fernandes, the captain of the ships and commander at sea. The tension can be seen in this entry from White's journal: "Simon Ferdinando [Fernandes] . . . lewdly forsook our . . . boat, leaving her distressed in the Bay of Portugal."

Harsh Conditions

Conditions on board the ships were harsh. Professor Karen Ordahl Kupperman of the University of Connecticut states that only the highest officers had individual bunks. The colonists and sailors slept on blankets on the floor between decks. The food was rancid and the water and other beverages, mostly wine and beer, spoiled after a month at sea. During storms the colonists stayed below decks where rats and cockroaches crawled over them. Seawater leaked into the ship and mixed with

"[Fernandes abandoned the colony] saying that the summer was far spent, wherefore he would land all the planters [on Roanoke Island]."

John White

"White may have been secretly pleased to be back on familiar ground."

Karen Ordahl Kupperman, associate professor of history at the University of Connecticut and author of *Roanoke: The Abandoned Colony*

vomit, feces, and urine, creating an unbearable stench.

After six arduous weeks, the two ships landed on the island of St. Croix in the Virgin Islands. The colonists, unaccustomed to long sea voyages, were grateful to be able to stretch their legs and collect fresh water.

Relations Are Strained

In the Caribbean, relations between White and Fernandes became strained again. White wanted to stop at one of the smaller islands to collect salt. Fernandes refused, saying that the ships might be damaged in the process. White's journal indicates that he believed Fernandes was not worried about the welfare of the ships but simply did not want to stop.

The conflict recurred when White wanted to stop at Puerto Rico to take some fruit plants for transplanting at the colony. Fernandes again refused. Because he did not keep a journal, we will never know his side of the story. It is possible, believe some historians, that Fernandes's lack of interest in the colony and his personal animosity for its leader may have contributed to the later disappearance of the colonists.

On July 22, 1587, the two ships arrived at Roanoke Island. The expedition leaders had planned that White and company would reunite with the fifteen colonists left the previous summer by Grenville and then go on to the new site at Chesapeake Bay.

Thus White and forty colonists boarded the smaller of the two ships and set out for the island. After they were on board, however, they were informed that Fernandes (on the larger ship) had ordered them dropped off at Roanoke Island and left there. Fernandes had determined that it was too late in the season to continue to Chesapeake. He knew that unloading the ships could take weeks, and he wanted to set sail for England as soon as possible.

White's journal indicates he believed that Fernandes wanted to raid some Spanish ships before the seas became too harsh with the advancing season. Fernandes himself made no secret of the fact that he found privateering more rewarding than colonization.

Settling in on Roanoke

In this way White found himself and his colonists on Roanoke Island, a place previously determined to be unsuitable for colonization. They set about finding the fifteen men left by Grenville. Instead they found the bones of one of the men, obviously slain by natives the previous autumn. They discovered no signs of the other fourteen men.

The next day White and the colonists, with no alternative so late in the year, began rebuilding

Although Gov. John White and the colonists thought Roanoke Island was unsuitable for colonization, natives thrived there. In this lithograph, natives cook fish at a camp near the island shore.

Lane's old fortress and buildings. They planned to move to a suitable location on Chesapeake Bay the next spring, as had been planned originally. The buildings had been unoccupied since the previous autumn. Melons were growing in the dirt floors, and deer grazed in the compound.

They began construction of new, smaller homes for the families. Thus commenced the second attempt to establish a colony on Roanoke Island.

Two days later they had some good news. The third ship, thought to have been lost off Portugal, arrived at the island with needed additional settlers and supplies.

Further Hostilities

Manteo, acting as an interpreter, attempted to discover the fate of Grenville's fifteen men. He spoke with some natives in the area. They were not his tribe, the Croatoans, but another local tribe known as the Roanoacs. They told him the Croatoans had moved to lands a few miles south after their mishaps with Grenville. Manteo also learned that the Roanoacs had attacked the fifteen colonists left on the island, killing one and chasing the rest away. It is not known what happened to these fourteen men. In a sense, these people are the first "lost colonists" of Roanoke Island.

None of the other colonists saw the Roanoacs during the first few days on the island and so believed that they were in no danger of attack. Then one day one of White's twelve assistants, George Howe, went out alone fishing for crabs in the waters off the island. He had taken off most of his clothes and laid them with his weapons on the bank. Roanoac natives concealed in nearby reeds attacked the defenseless man and killed him.

Anxious to prevent further hostilities, White, a man named Edward Stafford, and Manteo journeyed south to talk with the Croatoans, the people of Manteo and Wingina. They hoped to gain the

Natives were questioned about the fate of Grenville's fifteen men.

Croatoans' help in dealing with the Roanoacs. But the natives were understandably wary of the Englishmen, and on the first meeting they simply ran away when they saw the colonists approach. Manteo coaxed them back, and White, remembering Grenville's brutal treatment of Wingina's tribe, promised the natives that he had no intention of taking any food from them. White said, "Our coming was only to renew the old love that was between us and them at first, and to live with them as brethren and friends."

The natives were apparently still a trusting group. According to White, his remarks "seemed to please them well"—so well that they took the company back to their village and set out a feast for them.

White asked their leader to call all the chiefs in the area together. He wanted to make clear his peaceful intentions so that no more of his party would be slain. The chief said he would do his best to bring them to White's house at the settlement in seven days.

Rash Actions

White was impatient to hear from them. After a week had gone by, he decided that friendliness had failed. White devised a plan to attack the Roanoacs to demonstrate that the slaying of Howe would not be tolerated. David Stick, a modern-day historian who lives on the Outer Banks, says, "It was almost as though they had just finished reading Lane's account of his troubles with Wingina and decided to take a page from the soldier's journal." In other words, White and his men were about to make the same mistake that Lane and his soldiers had made.

Stick says, "The plan adopted was to send Captain Stafford, with Manteo serving as guide, across the sound [water passage between the island and the mainland] under cover of darkness to launch a surprise attack on the . . . [Roanoac] town of Dasamonguepeuc."

Some natives were wary of the English colonists and ran when they saw them.

In recognition of Manteo's loyalty to the English, Queen Elizabeth, pictured here, titled him "Lord of Roanoke."

The party landed near where the natives lay sleeping and moved into position between the water's edge and the natives. They attacked, catching the sleepy people by surprise. Those not killed instantly fled into some nearby high reeds.

A Horrible Mistake

The English closed in, readying for the final kill, when one of the natives called Captain Stafford's name. Stick says, "At almost the same time it became clear that one of the [natives] was carrying a child in a black sling." It was a young mother, not a fierce warrior. Stafford and his men had made a careless and horrible mistake. These people were not the Roanoacs responsible for the death of George Howe. They were Manteo's Croatoans who had traveled north from their home to join White for the meeting he had called. The Roanoacs had fled upon the death of Howe, fearing revenge by the English. Now, the Croatoans were gathering the food left behind the hasty retreat of the Roanoacs.

Manteo had unknowingly participated in the slaughter of his own innocent people.

Shortly afterwards, he was given the title Lord of Roanoke by Queen Elizabeth in recognition of his loyalty for remaining with the English despite their unintentional slaughter of his kin.

The Croatoans were generous enough to see the killing for the mistake it was. But White, like Grenville before him, had ruined his chances for wholehearted cooperation and trust between natives and colonists.

On August 18, an event took place that brought some happiness to the unlucky colony. A baby girl

Virginia Dare was the first English child born in the New World. Her baptism is recorded in this nineteenth-century lithograph.

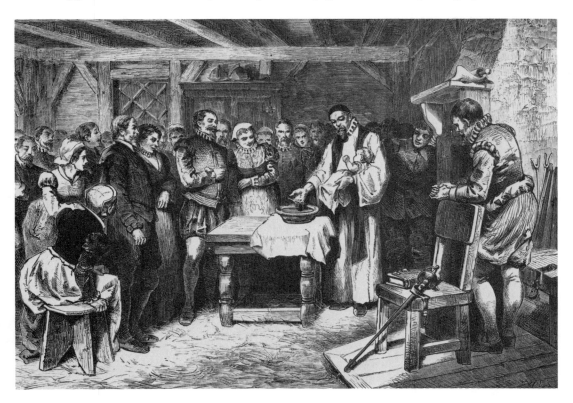

44

"[We told the natives that] our coming was only to renew the old love that was between us . . . and to live as brethren and friends."

John White

"[The natives,] in respect of troubling our inhabiting and planting, are not to be feared. They shall have cause to fear . . . us that shall inhabit with them."

Thomas Hariot, Raleigh's scientific adviser and participant in voyage of Amadas and Barlowe

was born to White's daughter, Eleanor White Dare. She was the first English child born in the new land. She was named Virginia in honor of that fact.

Difficult Decisions

During the month the colonists had been on the island, Simao Fernandes was anchored off the coast waiting for the time-consuming work of transporting the supplies and colonists from the ships to the settlement to be completed. By the end of August, he could wait no longer. With his departure imminent, the colony faced a dilemma. White and his assistants all agreed that one of them needed to go back to England to secure additional supplies for the colony, but no one wanted to go. His assistants thought White himself would have the greatest influence in England and wanted him to go. White refused, saying that it would not look good for him to return so quickly from Virginia, as if he had abandoned the colony. He was also worried about his possessions—a suit of armor, books, maps, and drawing supplies—being ruined in the move to the new site on Chesapeake Bay.

But his assistants eventually persuaded him to go. On August 27, 1587, White sailed in the smaller ship for England. Apparently he did not wish to spend the two-month journey with Fernandes.

White was optimistic about the chances for the colony's first winter on the island. He looked forward to returning in the spring and resuming his post as governor, perhaps arriving in time to supervise the move to the new location.

But White barely made it to England alive. An accident at sea injured twelve of his crew of fifteen men, virtually disabling the ship. In October the small ship encountered a storm that blew it far off course. The journey took much longer than expected, and food and water became scarce. White recorded in his journal that he expected "by famine to perish at sea."

But eventually, the crew, weakened by injury and hunger, landed on the coast of Ireland. Though White's return journey had been perilous, he had good news to bring back to Walter Raleigh. Raleigh was delighted that his brainchild, the City of Raleigh, had been founded. White and Raleigh optimistically set about obtaining supplies for the colonists at Roanoke. White had no way of knowing that he would never see the colonists, including his daughter and granddaughter, again.

The Spanish Armada

There would be no return voyage in six months as White had expected. Tensions with the Spanish had been increasing steadily during the time of England's efforts at colonization. In 1588, they reached a point of boiling over. The Spanish Armada—the huge Spanish fleet many years in construction—was about to sail against England. Queen Elizabeth ordered that all English ships discontinue their normal business and join the effort to fight. The very survival of England was in question.

Raleigh was diverted from his concerns about the colony, too. Queen Elizabeth had ordered him to see that the English coast was defended. He busied

Fearing war with Spain and its mighty Armada, Queen Elizabeth ordered English ships to discontinue their normal business and to battle Spanish vessels.

himself procuring enough soldiers and ammunition to defend the lengthy and vulnerable coastline.

Early in 1588, however, he found the time to write to his brother, who was in charge of assembling England's fleet. He asked that John White and two small boats be allowed to "steal away." And so John White was able to set sail in the spring of 1588 after all.

Unfortunately, the captain of the two vessels was more interested in privateering than in relieving the colonists. He picked a fight with two French warships more than twice the size of his own ships. He was forced to surrender, and the English ships full of supplies were looted. White returned to England alive, but he would have to wait more than a year before heading back to the colony.

According to David Stick, White returned to England the very same week thirty thousand Spanish soldiers in Lisbon, Portugal, were being pre-

Because Spanish ships were massive and carried large cannons, the Armada was thought to be invincible. But English ships proved more maneuverable and destroyed many Spanish ships, reducing the Spanish threat to England.

pared to go to sea against the English. A great naval battle took place shortly afterwards.

The Spanish Armada was thought to be invincible. However, Spanish ship designers had made the mistake of making the ships massive, with large guns. The English ships had smaller guns, but were also smaller in size and more maneuverable. As a result, the English were able to dart in, hit their targets with cannon fire, and dart out unharmed. In the summer of 1588, the English navy destroyed many Spanish ships and successfully defended England from invasion by the Spanish. Had the outcome been different, North Americans would be speaking Spanish today instead of English. Sir Walter Raleigh and Sir Francis Drake were two well-known privateers who were instrumental in the defeat of the Spanish. They both seemingly forgot about the English people in need of their help on the other side of the Atlantic Ocean.

More Difficulties

With the Spanish naval threat greatly reduced, White began preparing a relief ship for the colonists. But Raleigh's interest in the project had begun to wane. By 1589 he was devoting time to writing poetry and courting his future wife. He had always been a man with many projects going on at once, and perhaps after the defeat of the Spanish he wished to enjoy his life and wealth more.

Whatever the reason, White was forced to raise most of the money, ships, and supplies on his own. Because of that, he was not able to set sail until February 1590. Again the ships had a dual purpose: They carried supplies for the colonists, but they were also privateers. Therefore, they dallied in the Caribbean for several weeks until August 1590. It was then that they followed the smoke on the beach, searched the island, and found only the word Croatoan. The colony at Roanoke had become the Lost Colony.

Three

Did the Colonists Survive?

What happened to the colonists during the three years between White's visits? Did they prosper or did they starve? Did they get along well with the natives, or poorly? Did they move to Croatoan as the message on the tree suggested? If so, was it because they wanted to go or because circumstances forced them to go?

Using the limited information available, scholars and historians have tried to piece together what happened after the colonists were left alone in a strange land. The experts do not all reach the same conclusions.

The Move to Croatoan

Stephen B. Weeks, a historian who wrote around the turn of the twentieth century, thought the colonists left Roanoke Island shortly after Governor White departed in the late summer of 1587. By then, it was too late to plant crops, so Weeks believes the colonists either moved to Croatoan that fall or stayed on the island and lived off the food and supplies they had brought with them until the following spring.

Weeks believed the reason Governor White was not able to locate the colonists three years later was that the word *Croatoan* was too vague. It referred to

(opposite page) At times, the colonists and natives got along well. Here, Capt. John Smith amuses native girls with a toy.

> "Historians . . . have been saying for hundreds of years that the descendants of the lost colonists were alive and well in North Carolina."
>
> Adolph Dial, chairman of the Department of American Indian Studies, Pembroke State University, North Carolina, and a Hatteras Indian

> "[Captain John Smith of Jamestown] has specific admissions from Powhatan that he had killed the lost colonists."
>
> David Beers Quinn, historian and professor at University of Liverpool

a huge area of land used by the Croatoan, or Hatteras, tribe. The Croatoan area with which Grenville, Lane, and White were familiar was an island in the Outer Banks that lay to the south of Roanoke Island. But Croatoan territory was much more extensive. Weeks and other historians believe the island was an unlikely destination for the colony. It was barren and sandy, unable to support significant plant life. The colonists would not have been able to raise crops there. Not only was it unsuitable for agriculture, it was also exposed to the sea. A colony located there would have been easy prey for Spanish ships. Weeks thought it unlikely that the colonists would leave Roanoke Island for such a place.

He believed that the Croatoan area that the colonists moved to was the peninsula of Dasamonguepeuc, located on the mainland to the east of Roanoke Island. The Croatoan tribe used this large area for hunting and gathering food.

Wholly Integrated

Weeks suggested this scenario: The spring of 1588 arrived without sign of White or supplies and reinforcements from England. As time passed, the colonists lost faith in the return of their countrymen. They also increasingly mingled with their Croatoan hosts, eventually becoming wholly integrated with the tribe.

David Beers Quinn, professor of history at the University of Liverpool and author of numerous books on British colonialism in North America, also believes that if the colonists survived, they would have integrated into native society quickly. Although White's colony included some families, men still far outnumbered women. Eighty-five men, seventeen women, and eleven children were left on Roanoke Island. If the Croatoan society allowed it, Quinn reckons that English men would have started pairing up with native women within four or five years of 1587. The two groups, English and Croatoan, would have continued to integrate, especially after half-Croatoan, half-English children were born. Eventually, they would have blended into one.

Early Clues

Is there any evidence to support this theory? Weeks found several reports from later settlers in North America that seem to do so.

The first tells of an incident that took place in May of 1607, nineteen years after White left the colonists. Another colony, called the Virginia Company, was underway north of Roanoke in Jamestown. A member of that colony, George Percy, spotted a native "boy about the age of ten years. . . . [He had] hair of a perfect yellow and . . . white skin." While it was not impossible that a full-blooded Croatoan native had fair skin and blonde hair, it was highly unlikely. It is more likely that this boy had some European blood, that one of his

Some historians believe the colonists could have adopted the native lifestyle. Here, natives fish the waters off Roanoke Island.

parents was English.

Three years later a report by Jamestown colonists included rumors of some of the people "planted by Sir Walter Raleigh, yet alive, within fifty miles of our fort." No one from the Jamestown colony ever made contact with the lost colonists, although a few saw crosses and letters carved in trees. This suggests that English people lived somewhere in the area, and Quinn calls the carvings "reminiscent of the signs left for White in 1590."

The Lost Colonists

Capt. John Smith of the Jamestown colonists recorded similar stories and rumors. He wrote that a native leader told him of a group of people at a place called Ocanahonan located near Roanoke Island. The native described "certain men . . . clothed like me [Smith]." This suggests that Europeans were probably present in the area. Also, the area described as Ocanahonan sounds very near the area Weeks called Croatoan. If this is true, then there is a good chance that those people were the lost colonists.

William Strachey was another member of the Virginia Company who kept a record of rumors he heard from the natives of the area. He reported, "At Peccarecamek and Ochanahoen . . . the people have houses built with stone walls, and one story built upon another, so taught them by those English [of the Roanoke colony]." No native tribes of the East Coast of North America were building stone buildings at that time, and certainly none of them built structures of more than one level. Both of those characteristics were typical of European dwellings. This also supports the theory that the lost colonists were living with a native tribe in the area.

The next evidence of possible English influence among the native people can be found in a 1704 report by a missionary traveling around the present-day Albemarle Sound. Rev. John Blair told of a powerful tribe "computed to be no less than one

These actors dramatize the pioneering spirit of the early English colonists.

How they took him prisoner in the Ooze 1607

C. Smith bindeth a saluage to his arme, fighteth with the King of Pamaunkee and all his company, and slew 3 of them.

Capt. John Smith learned through a native leader that some of the colonists may have been seen near Roanoke Island.

hundred thousand, many of which live amongst the English." This report continued the legend of a mixed English and native community. Blair did not meet any members of this huge community, however. All his information was secondhand.

Around that same time, the first historian of North Carolina, a man named John Lawson, was interviewing the Hatteras (Croatoan) natives on the Croatoan Island. They told him stories about their white ancestors. They said that "their ancestors were white people and could . . . [read] as we do, the truth of which is confirmed by grey eyes being found frequently amongst these Indians and no others." Lawson believed, as did George Percy in 1607, that the typically white features of the natives

Despite reports of violence between natives and colonists, some historians today believe the groups integrated. This would explain the disappearance of the lost colonists.

were evidence of European ancestry. Also, the practice of reading showed European influence.

On the basis of this information, Lawson concluded that the white ancestors of the Hatteras were the lost colonists. He speculated that "the settlement miscarried for want of timely supplies from England; or through the treachery of the natives, for we may reasonably suppose that the English were forced to cohabit with them . . . and that in the process of time they conformed themselves to the manners of their Indian relations." Lawson was the first historian to articulate the theory that the colonists of Roanoke went to live with the natives in order to survive and that the colonists integrated into native society.

Today a tribe called the Lumbees maintain that they are descended from the Hatteras, or Croatoan, people. They also continue to hold the traditional belief that they are descendants of the lost colonists.

Similar Speech

In the 1890s Stephen Weeks saw similarities between the distinctive speech of the Lumbees and the sixteenth-century English that would have been spoken by the settlers of Roanoke. When Weeks interviewed them, the Lumbees' pronunciation and word use were different from both the whites and the African-Americans around them. For example, Weeks reported that the Lumbees pronounced the word "father" like an Irishman of the sixteenth century might have, *fayther*. For *knowledge*, they said "wit." This is a sixteenth-century usage of the word. It can be seen used that way in the plays of Shakespeare. The Lumbees' language preserved many characteristics in use in the sixteenth century that had long since passed out of use everywhere else.

Weeks also heard stories of the Lumbees' white ancestors. They told Weeks that their former home was Roanoke Island. They referred to North Carolina as Virginia, as it was called when the English first arrived. They spoke to Weeks about a native leader called "Maino" or "Mainor." Weeks believed this may have been a variation on the name of Manteo.

Perhaps most convincing to Weeks was the fact that many of the Lumbees have surnames the same as or similar to those of the lost colonists. It is unusual for Native Americans to have English and Irish names, even if the names are fairly common. Yet surnames such as Scott, Taylor, and Martin can be found on both the original list of colonists left on Roanoke Island and among the Lumbees of Weeks' time and today. Weeks said that when he told an old man the story of Virginia Dare the man said that he recognized the story, but that her name probably

"There is overwhelming evidence that . . . the colonists . . . joined friendly Indians [the Hatteras] and eventually intermarried with them."

Adolph Dial, chairman of the Department of American Indian Studies, Pembroke State University, North Carolina, and a Hatteras Indian

"There were other opportunities for an admixture of the races [between Europeans and Hatteras]."

Samuel A'Court Ashe, a historian of the late nineteenth and early twentieth centuries survived as *Darr*, *Durr*, or *Dorr*.

A nineteenth-century historian named Hamilton MacMillan also believed the Lumbees are descended from the lost colonists. In 1885 he convinced members of the North Carolina legislature to grant the Lumbees special status under law on that basis. The Lumbees were allowed to have their own schools and community buildings. In those days of poor treatment of racial and ethnic minorities in the United States, the Lumbees were treated better than most Native American tribes, presumably because of their white ancestry.

Evidence Is Shaky

Many prominent historians have looked at the same evidence Weeks and MacMillan did but do not accept the idea that the lost colonists joined the Lumbee tribe. Samuel A'Court Ashe, for example, was a nineteenth-century historian who wrote around the same time Stephen Weeks did. Ashe agreed that the fair-skinned, blonde boy seen in the woods in 1607 was probably of European descent. But he thought there were several opportunities for natives to mix with Europeans. Both the Spanish and the French may have passed through that area at different times. Also, the fifteen men abandoned by Grenville in 1585 were never found. Perhaps they joined some native tribe and intermarried. There are many possibilities.

Twentieth-century historian David Beers Quinn believes that the tale about the two-story houses is probably more fiction than fact. He points out that Strachey's text is based on legend and not personal observation.

Quinn also believes that the men clothed like Europeans who were reported by John Smith of the Virginia Company were probably Frenchmen who colonized the St. Lawrence seaway at that time. Quinn concluded that Smith's limited knowledge of the native language, Algonquian, caused him to confuse the words for "north" and "south." In so doing, he thought that the French to the north of Jamestown were English to the south.

Both Ashe and Quinn thought unreliable the reports made in 1704 by John Blair, the traveling missionary, of the large mixed tribe of native and white people. Samuel A'Court Ashe stated that the Hatteras tribe was said to be very small, less than two hundred people, before *and* after the time the colonists would have joined. If that is true, then the missionary's report of a tribe of "no less than one hundred thousand" is a gross exaggeration. Such a large discrepancy calls into question the accuracy of all of Blair's information.

Quinn thinks Ashe's figures are too low, but Blair's are far too high. He believes the Hatteras tribe must have been over one thousand people at the time the colonists landed at Roanoke. If Quinn

Since 1896, people have visited the monument to the Lost Colony of Roanoke.

Members of the Hatteras tribe may have sought to isolate themselves from the colonists by moving deep into the North Carolina swamps (above).

is right, another issue arises: It seems unrealistic to think that the European culture would have been so influential on so large a tribe. If there were one hundred Hatteras for every colonist, why would the natives bother to take English surnames? Why would members of a thriving society change the way they built their homes?

Whether the missionary's report is accepted or rejected, it seems inadequate to back up a theory that the Roanoke colonists joined the Hatteras tribe. Even Weeks, who cited the missionary's report, admits that it is "very vague and indefinite." The problem with using historical data such as that cited above is that it is often incomplete or unsupported.

The Hatteras Today

But what about the present-day Hatteras tribe? Are their sixteenth-century English speech patterns, English surnames, and legends of descent from the lost colonists proof that the lost colonists were assimilated by them? Some historians would again answer with an emphatic "no."

The legends of the Lumbees' English ancestors are interesting but prove nothing, just as the legend of Paul Bunyan does not prove that a fifty-foot-tall man and a massive blue ox really roamed the northern United States. And while the large number of surnames similar to those of the lost colonists is compelling, Samuel A'Court Ashe pointed out that these names were fairly common English and Irish surnames and could have been picked up at any time between the sixteenth and nineteenth centuries.

Ashe also believed that the Hatteras would not have taken the English surnames if the colonists *did* join them. He wrote that it would have been "highly improbable" that English names would have lasted "beyond the second generation, there being no communication except with other [natives]." There would have been no need for the English surnames because there was no need for surnames at all. Thus, it would be unlikely for them to survive to the present.

Also, Samuel A'Court Ashe asked why it took until the nineteenth century for the surnames to be noticed if they had been in place for three hundred years. Adolph Dial, a modern-day Lumbee who believes he is a descendant of Virginia Dare, argues that the colonists and the Hatteras tribe both had reason to isolate themselves from a common enemy. They sought isolation in the swamps of North Carolina. They could easily have been unnoticed by historians for hundreds of years.

Ashe agreed that the physical location of the tribe may have isolated it from all contact until the nineteenth century. Or perhaps contact was made, but the record of it was subsequently lost or destroyed. The evidence, then, can be seen to *support* the theory but does not prove it.

An Untimely Destiny

In fact, the theory that the colonists joined the Hatteras tribe, thrived, and continue to live today is far from being accepted. Quinn and Ashe, for example, agree with the report of William Strachey written around 1620, in which he concludes that "the poor planters [colonists] . . . came . . . to a miserable and untimely destiny."

> "Those people had—and their descendants still have—English family names that were exactly the same as the lost colonists had, such as Brooks, Sampson, and Jones."
>
> Adolph Dial, chairman of the Department of American Indian Studies, Pembroke State University, North Carolina, and a Hatteras Indian

> "Whatever may have been . . . the origin of their English names, neither the names nor their English manners could have been perpetuated from the time of the lost colony without exciting some remark on the part of explorers or historians. Apparently that community came into being at a later date."
>
> John Lawson, nineteenth-century historian of North Carolina

Four

Were the Colonists Murdered?

Is it possible that the colonists did not survive after they lost contact with White and the English? Certainly the new land held many dangers: animals, storms, disease, and hostile natives. Some historians believe that it was the last of these, hostile natives, that prematurely ended the colonists' lives. One such historian is David Beers Quinn.

The Colony Splits

Quinn's theory begins with what is known: White left the colony late in 1587 for supplies, promising to return the following year. Then, Quinn believes, the people who were left behind agreed to split up. Most of them went to live on the shores of Chesapeake Bay to the north, the intended site of the so-called City of Raleigh. They decided to haul their possessions there and set up some buildings before the winter began.

But not everyone could go. Some had to stay on Roanoke Island to meet White and take him and the supplies to the new settlement. Quinn estimates that about twenty-five men stayed behind. That means about sixty men, seventeen women, one girl, and ten boys left to create the permanent settlement on Chesapeake Bay.

(opposite page) Did hostile natives massacre the lost colonists of Roanoke?

"At about the time Jamestown was founded, [Powhatan] attacked and wiped out the Chesapeakes, including their English members."

Karen Ordahl Kupperman, associate professor of history at the University of Connecticut and author of *Roanoke: The Abandoned Colony*

"Q: Why is there still a widespread idea that the lost colony was wiped out? Dial: It suits the purpose of some romantics who are more intrigued by a supposedly unsolved mystery than the facts."

Adolph Dial, chairman of Department of American Indian Studies at Pembroke State University, North Carolina, and a Hatteras Indian

Quinn believes the site they chose was near a village of the friendly Chesapeake tribe. The native village probably contained a thousand people or more. The colonists planned to live off the supplies of food brought with them as well as the corn and game available locally, until they could plant and harvest crops of their own. Also, the Chesapeake were better able to supply the colonists than were the Croatoans. The area was much more fertile than coastal North Carolina and game much more plentiful. The colonists reassured the tribe of their friendly intentions. They demonstrated their plan to grow their own crops and not rely on the Chesapeakes for an eternal food supply as the 1585 settlement had relied on Wingina's people.

A Boatslip Sighted

Spanish documents from the period note that a boatslip was sighted on Chesapeake Bay in 1588. This suggests that settlers had already been there for at least a few months. Quinn believes construction of the City of Raleigh had been begun by that time. The boatslip was built, probably at least in part, to accommodate the relief ships expected from John White. When he did not show up by late 1588, no doubt the settlers began to question whether he would show up at all.

That doubt must also have been felt by the party waiting on Roanoke Island. Lack of evidence of some kind of permanent settlement indicates that they left the island before the winter of 1588-89. Quinn suggests that the group of twenty or so men moved south to Croatoan to live with Manteo and Granganimeo's people, the friendly Croatoan tribe. They would have been running out of food and other supplies and would not have been able to survive another winter on their own. Perhaps they thought White might show up the following spring and find them at nearby Croatoan; then both groups could have proceeded to the Chesapeake Bay site.

On this hope, they carved the word *Croatoan* into the tree and departed.

Quinn says we will never know for sure. But we can be certain that as the months passed with no sign of White or the English ships, the colonists must have resigned themselves to their situation. As far as the colonists knew, White would not return.

Quinn believes both groups of colonists would have begun to integrate into the native communities. The larger group would have moved their dwellings into the Chesapeake tribe's village area. They would have cultivated the fields, hunted, and woven alongside the Chesapeakes. The other group, being smaller and comprised entirely of men, must have been eager to join the Croatoan tribe once it became apparent that no English reinforcements would arrive. The only alternative for those twenty-five men would have been to live in lonely isolation.

So, Quinn believes, in the 1590s both groups of colonists were well and alive. They had food, shel-

When Gov. John White found "CROATOAN" carved into the bark of a tree, did he think the colonists had joined native tribes?

ter, and companionship. Legends from both tribes, Croatoan and Chesapeake, indicate that both accepted the white people, lived peaceably alongside them, and eventually intermixed.

The Powhatan Tribe

Besides the Chesapeake and the Croatoan, many more tribes lived in the area. One particularly powerful one that may have affected the colonists' destinies was called the Powhatan tribe, named for its strong and ambitious ruler. Many historians, including Quinn, believe the Powhatan tribe contained remnants of the Roanoacs, Wingina's tribe slain by Lane in 1586.

Powhatan was a fierce leader at the end of the sixteenth century. Through diplomacy and war, he gained control over most of the tribes around him. One tribe he did not dominate was the Chesapeake. Its size would have cost him too many warriors to take by force. According to Quinn, he knew the tribe contained the English from Raleigh's lost colony, but he did not bother them.

In 1603, however, something happened that may have begun to make Powhatan suspicious of the English. An English exploratory mission sailed into Chesapeake Bay seeking a suitable location for another colony, to be called Jamestown. The English met some natives along the shoreline. To learn firsthand about the area, they kidnapped the natives and took them back to England. Those captured were Powhatan's men. When Powhatan was told what had happened, he probably began to wonder about the intentions of these white-skinned people toward his territory. Yet he took no action.

The colonists at Chesapeake continued to live as they had been. As more time passed, they became further and further integrated into the Chesapeake society. As Quinn put it, "Their Englishness would be wearing thin."

Sometime around 1605, Powhatan's priests, or

"[Sixteenth-century historian William Strachey] believed that the Roanoke colonists somehow survived among the Indians, only to be murdered some twenty years later by Powhatan at the behest of shamans."

Bernard W. Sheehan, professor at Indiana University and historian

"It is now believed that the colonists of 1587 removed to Croatoan soon after the return of Governor White to England; that they intermarried with the . . . Hatteras Indians; that their wanderings westward can be definitely traced, and that their descendants can be identified today."

Stephen B. Weeks, nineteenth-century historian

iniocasockes, prophesied that some group would threaten his power if he did not stop them. According to William Strachey of the Jamestown colony, "His priests told him . . . that from the Chesapeake Bay a nation should arise which would dissolve and give end to his empire." Given such a forecast, Powhatan must have become increasingly nervous about the foreigners who lived near Chesapeake Bay. And indeed, by the time the Jamestown colony was established, he had taken action against them, which he later described to Englishman John Smith.

Massacre at Chesapeake?

In April 1607, the Virginia Company sailed its ships into Chesapeake Bay. Jamestown was to be a massive permanent colony. It was better funded than Raleigh's colony. The Jamestown colonists had instructions to look for the lost colonists, if time permitted. Certainly there was much for the Jamestown colonists to do: unloading the ships, building houses and community buildings, hunting, and planting crops. On the other hand, there was great interest among the Jamestown settlers in finding the lost colonists. If found, they could have shared twenty years worth of valuable experience.

It is probable that Powhatan took the presence of English ships as a sign that the prophecy of his priests was coming true. Powhatan did not take any chances. According to Strachey, Powhatan "put to [the] sword all such that might . . . [fit the criteria] of the said prophecy. . . . And so remain all the *Chessiopeians* [Chesapeake] at this day, and for this cause, extinct." In other words, Strachey said, Powhatan killed off the entire tribe of Chesapeake as well as the lost colonists and mixed-race children because he feared that the English would take over his territory.

Shortly after the massacre, the Virginia Company landed and went ashore. That night, April 26, 1607, natives attacked the company. They injured

Did Powhatan order his people to kill the colonists because he feared a takeover by the English?

Some historians believe Powhatan (seated) sent his own warriors to attack the settlers.

several English before they were dispersed by gunfire. Gabriel Archer, a Jamestown colonist, reported that one of Powhatan's sons later came to greet them and told them that they had been attacked by the Chesapeake tribe. Archer believed what he was told and "took occasion to signify our displeasure with them [the Chesapeakes] also."

But Quinn notes that the Chesapeake tribe was already extinct by this time. He theorizes that Powhatan sent his own warriors to attack the settlers. When the attack was unsuccessful, he blamed the Chesapeakes, thereby drawing the colonists' wrath away from his own tribe. The attack also prevented the English from trying to meet the Chesapeakes and thus reduced the chance that they would discover Powhatan's slaughter. Powhatan's son must have been very happy when Archer indicated that the English would stay away from the Chesapeakes. The trick had worked beautifully.

Strange Leavings

The next day the Virginia Company went inland to find a site for settlement and to explore the area. They found things there that puzzled them. One was an open space of land. George Percy, a member of the company, wrote that they "went on land and found the place five miles in [size] without either bush or tree." Such a large, clear area would have been unlikely to occur naturally. Yet the settlers saw no natives tilling the soil or living nearby.

The group proceeded inland and saw the "great smoke of [a] fire." They believed that it had been set by a group of natives. The group later passed tilled land, including "a little plot of ground full of fine and beautiful strawberries." But they still saw no sign of native life. Could the fire have been used to cover up signs of a massacre? Could the fields have been used by the Chesapeake tribe for agriculture before the people were cleared from the area by Powhatan?

As Jamestown became established, the settlers

had more time to attend to other concerns. One of those was finding the lost colonists. In 1608 and the following year, search parties were organized and sent out. They found very little. They were told vague stories by Powhatan about a group of men to the south. So they began their search around the Chowan River area where the settlers of 1585-86 had explored. Quinn believes that Powhatan's story about the white men to the south was "a mere tale" designed to lead the Virginia Company away from the lost colonists and any evidence of them. Indeed, according to Smith, they found nothing. He wrote, "Nothing could we learn but [that] they were all dead." The Virginia Company did not yet suspect Powhatan of any deceit or foul play.

In fact, Powhatan had appeared to be friendly and helpful towards the Jamestown colonists. In recognition of this fact, King James had sent him a crown and an official title in 1608. Powhatan was to be a sub-king of the region, a ruler of the native people second only to King James himself.

But later that same year, Powhatan made a startling confession to Smith. According to Samuel Purchas, who wrote about the English colonies in 1623, "Powhatan confessed to Captain Smith that he had been at their [the lost colonists] slaughter." Again in 1625 Purchas wrote, "Powhatan confessed that he had been at the murder of [the lost] colony and showed to Captain Smith a musket barrel and a bronze mortar [a short-barreled cannon] and certain pieces of iron that had been theirs."

An Awkward Position

Quinn believes that a year earlier in 1607 when he was captured and held briefly by Powhatan, Smith may have suspected that Powhatan was connected to the fate of the colonists but had done nothing about his suspicions. Now, in 1608, he had a full confession and it placed him in an awkward position.

On one hand he faced an obvious enemy.

"The colonists were probably attacked at quite an early stage by hostile Indians."

Raleigh biographer Robert Lacey

"The Croatoans of today claim decent from the lost colony. Their habits, disposition, and mental characteristics show traces of both savage [native] and civilized [European] ancestry."

Stephen B. Weeks, nineteenth-century historian

Powhatan had presided over the merciless slaughter of other English colonists. On the other hand, he was dealing with a fellow servant of King James, and one of high rank. Smith proceeded cautiously. He sent word of his discoveries back to King James in a confidential memorandum and awaited the royal reaction to the news. Meanwhile, he concealed what he knew from the colonists at Jamestown.

King James solved his problem by blaming the slaughter not on Powhatan but on his priests. In instructions sent to the colony in 1609, but not arriving until a year later, the king told Smith to "remove from them their *iniocasockes* or priests by a surprise of them all and detaining them prisoners." The instructions did not tell Smith to kill the priests, but they indicated that such an outcome would have been acceptable. They read, "We pronounce it not cruelty nor breach of charity to deal more sharply with them and proceed even to death with these murderers of souls and sacrificers . . . to the devil."

Clues

Hints of the lost colonists continued to present themselves. The most intriguing was found in a 1609 report presented to the Royal Council for Virginia in England. The report described a possible future settlement site near the Roanoke and Chowan rivers. The report states that near this site, "you will find four of the English alive, left by Sir Walter Raleigh, which escaped from the slaughter of Powhatan of Roanoke upon the first arrival of our colony." They reportedly lived under the protection of a chief called Gepanocon. Because they were helping the chief smelt copper he was not willing to release them to the English. The natives did not know how to make copper, so the Englishmen's skills would have been valuable to Gepanocon.

While the report seems to prove that Englishmen were living in a native society, it cannot be assumed that they were lost colonists who survived the massacre. Quinn points out that they could be four of the men deserted by Lane in 1586. Those four people, like the lost colonists, remain a mystery.

The evidence presented by Quinn supports the theory that the lost colonists joined the Chesapeake tribe, lived with them for twenty years, and were killed by Powhatan as the Jamestown settlers sailed into Chesapeake Bay. However, even Quinn admits that his theory is only one possibility. It is far from being proven. He writes, "The deduction of such a story . . . would not be an illegitimate use of the evidence. On the other hand, it is clearly not the whole story, and it may be incorrect." In other words, Quinn feels that he has presented the best explanation of the available evidence. However, there may be other explanations and the evidence is at best incomplete.

An example of another theory derived from the same evidence is that of Stephen Weeks. Weeks believed that all the colonists went to Croatoan after White left. They lived there for twenty years until they heard of the Virginia Company's arrival. Anxious to rejoin their fellow English, most of them moved northward towards Jamestown. En route, they encountered Powhatan's warriors, who killed them, presumably for entering his territory uninvited. Those few that remained behind integrated with the Croatoan people.

Weeks used the same evidence that Quinn did but they arrived at different conclusions. Until more is known, whether or not the colonists were killed by Powhatan will be a mystery.

The Croatoan Group

Also a mystery is the fate of that smaller group of twenty-five colonists who stayed behind on Roanoke Island and then moved to Croatoan. They were far enough away from Powhatan's sphere of command that they would have escaped slaughter. Logically, then, could it be deduced that these men were the ancestors of the Lumbee people?

Powhatan told Capt. John Smith (above) that he had witnessed natives murdering the colonists.

Some historians believe that after Gov. John White left for England, the colonists went to Croatoan. Here, White is portrayed by an actor.

The integration of twenty-five men into the Lumbee tribe would not account for the claims made by Adolph Dial and Stephen Weeks. Twenty-five people would not be enough to change the speech patterns of the Croatoan tribe to the sixteenth-century English found by Stephen Weeks. Both Weeks and Dial noted more than twenty-five similar names between the original colonists and the Lumbees. Dial's claim that he was a descendant of Virginia Dare would have to be discounted. Virginia Dare would have been an infant when the two groups of colonists split. It is unlikely that her family would have left her behind on the island to endure the difficult conditions with the men.

Of Cherokee Descent?

Finally, no one has conclusively proven that the Lumbee tribe of today is even the same Croatoan tribe that lived near the lost colony of Roanoke. Angus W. McLean, a U.S. senator and governor of North Carolina, wrote in 1913 that the Lumbees were descended from the Cherokee tribe, not the Croatoan. He wrote: "Long before historians began to study the origins of these people they claimed to be of Cherokee descent. In fact, they have always claimed that they were originally a part of the Cherokee tribe and that they gave up their tribal relation after they had participated with the white man in the war against the Tuscaroras."

Many of the Lumbees also believe they are descended from the Cherokee. One middle-aged native said, "When I was coming up [growing up], we went by another name—Cherokee—but that wasn't good enough for some, so they changed it." It is obvious that the origins of the Lumbee tribe are not known for certain.

A Great Mystery

The lost colonists are truly lost. Many opposing and interesting theories speculate about what happened to them. No theory definitively answers the question "What happened to the women, men, and children John White left at Roanoke Island in 1587?" The stories found among the Lumbee tribe of their descent are compelling, yet the origin of the tribe itself can be questioned. Quinn's theory explains a lot of the evidence available, but that evidence is incomplete. New evidence could radically change the way the fate of the colonists is understood. Also, Quinn makes no attempt to account for the coincidence of names, speech, and traditions of the Lumbee tribe. On the other hand, Dial and Weeks made no attempt to account for reports that Powhatan killed the colonists of Roanoke.

Perhaps some day evidence will be discovered that will explain exactly what happened to the lost colonists. Perhaps the mystery will be solved to everyone's satisfaction. Quinn hopes that archaeologists, people who study the life and culture of ancient peoples by excavation of ancient cities and artifacts, will find a site with evidence of the lost colonists. Such a discovery might prove a present theory true or create a new one. Until that time, however, the fate of the colonists of Roanoke will remain a mystery.

"The men, women, and children of the first plantation at Roanoke [the lost colony] were by practize [sic] and commandment of Powhatan (he himself persuaded thereunto by his priests) miserably slaughtered."

William Strachey, Jamestown colonist writing in 1613

"[The colonists] were met by emissaries of Powhatan and some were slain. . . . Others were protected and saved by a chief named Eyanoco, who was probably connected in some way with the Croatoan tribe."

Stephen B. Weeks, nineteenth-century historian

Epilogue

What Conclusions Can Be Drawn?

It could be said that the colonies at Roanoke were doomed from the start. The first colony was supposed to contain 300 soldier-colonists, yet less than 110 stayed the winter. And Lane's diplomatic tactics almost got these people killed.

In establishing the second colony, White repeated Lane's mistakes almost exactly. Ironically, if the colonists survived, it may have been the natives who enabled them to do so. In retrospect, some would say the colonies of Roanoke Island represent a lesson in how *not* to establish settlements in a new land.

Evidence Is Lost

What exactly happened to the colonists remains unclear. The available historical evidence is incomplete and inconclusive. Like the colonists themselves, the evidence needed to settle the question of their fate is lost. The search continues: in the soil of New England; among historical documents in England and Spain; in the journals of sailors, soldiers, and royalty. Perhaps someday that elusive evidence will be discovered. But equally likely is that the evidence is lost forever, destroyed by time and nature. It is possible that the fate of the lost colonists will forever be unknown.

(opposite page) Today, actors dramatize the encounters between colonists and natives during the time of the Lost Colony of Roanoke.

For Further Exploration

Thomas Hariot, *A Brief and True Report of the New Found Land of Virginia*, facsimile reproduction of 1588 text. New York: History Book Club Press, 1951.

Stefan Lorant, *The New World: The First Pictures of America*. New York: Duell, Sloan, and Pierce, 1965.

David Beers Quinn, *Set Fair for Roanoke: Voyages and Colonies, 1584-1606*. Chapel Hill and London: University of North Carolina Press, 1984.

David Stick, *Roanoke Island*. Chapel Hill and London: University of North Carolina Press, 1983.

Works Consulted

Samuel A'Court Ashe, *History of North Carolina.* Greensboro, NC: Charles L. Van Noppen Publisher, 1908.

Karen I. Blu, *The Lumbee Problem.* New York and Cambridge: Press Syndicate of the University of Cambridge, 1980.

Sir Julian S. Corbett, *Drake and the Tudor Navy.* London: Longmans, Green, and Company, 1917.

Adolph Dial and David K. Eliades, *The Only Land I Know: A History of the Lumbee Indians.* San Francisco: The Indian Historian Press, 1975.

The Encyclopedia Americana, v. 23, pp. 239-240. Danbury, CT: Grolier Incorporated, 1989.

The First Colonists: Hakluyt's Voyages to North America. London: The Folio Society, 1986.

Great Soviet Encyclopedia, v. 22, p. 94. New York: MacMillan, Inc., 1979.

Karen Ordahl Kupperman, "Roanoke Lost," *American Heritage*, v. 36, n. 5, August/September 1985.

Robert Lacey, *Sir Walter Raleigh.* New York: Atheneum, 1974.

William MacDougall, "Happy 400th Birthday to America's English Settlers," *U.S. News & World Report*, July 9, 1984.

David Beers Quinn, *England and the Discovery of America, 1481-1620.* New York: Alfred A. Knopf, 1974.

David Beers Quinn, *Set Fair for Roanoke: Voyages and Colonies, 1584-1606*. Chapel Hill and London: University of North Carolina Press, 1984.

Edward Dwight Salmon, *Imperial Spain: The Rise of the Empire and the Dawn of Modern Sea Power.* New York: Henry Holt and Company, 1971 reprint.

Barnard W. Sheehan, *Savagism and Civility: Indians and Englishmen in Colonial Virginia.* Cambridge and London: Cambridge University Press, 1980.

David Stick, *Roanoke Island*. Chapel Hill and London: University of North Carolina Press, 1983.

Stephen B. Weeks, "The Lost Colony of Roanoke: Its Fate and Survival," *Papers of the American Historical Association.* New York and London: G.P. Putnam's Sons, 1891.

Roger Whiting, *The Enterprise of England: The Spanish Armada.* New York: St. Martin's Press, 1988.

Index

About the Author

Tom Schouweiler is a free-lance writer who was raised in Marine on St. Croix, Minnesota. He currently lives in St. Paul, Minnesota.

Schouweiler is inspired by the bravery of the Roanoke colonists, interested in their story, and fascinated by the possibility that they may have lived out their natural lives at a time when North America was a mystery to most of the world.

Picture Credits

Photos supplied by Research Plus, Inc., Mill Valley, California.

AP/Wide World Photos, 21, 31, 58

The Bettmann Archive, 35, 63

Dare Co. Tourist Bureau, 52, 70, 73

Historical Pictures Service, Chicago, 17, 36, 45, 46

Library of Congress, 9, 10, 15, 18 (both), 19, 20, 22, 24, 42, 43, 49, 53, 54, 61, 65, 66, 69

State Department of Cultural Resources, Raleigh, North Carolina, 12, 23, 28, 29, 32, 39, 40, 41, 51, 57

HQJN 626303
Schouweiler, Tom,
J   The lost colony of
975.6175   Roanoke : opposing
SCHOU